MW00427150

SOUP! SOUP! SOUP!

CHINESE STYLE

湯

AUTHOR
Mu-Tsun Lee

EDITOR
Huang Su-Huei

EDITORIAL STAFF
Sophia Lin
Yen-Jen Lai
John Holt

TRANSLATION
Innie Hua

ART DIRECTION
F.S. Chang

PHOTOGRAPHY
Aki Ohno

DESIGN
AGP Productions Inc.

WEI-CHUAN PUBLISHING
1455 Monterey Pass Rd., #110
Monterey Park, CA 91754, U.S.A.
Tel: (213)261-3880 (213)261-3878
Fax: (213)261-3299

2nd Fl., 28 Section 4, Jen-Ai Road
Taipei, Taiwan, R.O.C.
Tel: (02)702-1148 (02)702-1149
Fax: (02)704-2729

PRINTED IN TAIWAN, R.O.C.

FIRST PRINTING, OCTOBER 1994
ISBN 0-941676-50-1

作者
李木村

總編輯
黃淑惠

文稿協助
林淑華、賴燕眞、何久恩

翻譯
華茵

設計策劃
張方馨

攝影
大野現

設計
AGP Productions Inc.

電腦排版
甘露資訊印刷有限公司

印刷
中華彩色印刷股份有限公司

味全出版社有限公司
台北市仁愛路4段28號2樓
郵政劃撥00182038號味全出版社帳戶
電話： (02) 702-1148. (02) 702-1149
傳眞： (02) 704-2729

版權所有
局版台業字第0179號
中華民國83年10月初版
定價：新台幣壹佰貳拾元整

Contents 目 錄

Conversion Tables 量器介紹

1 C. (1 cup) = 236 c.c.   1杯 = 236 c.c.

1 T. (1 tablespoon) = 15 c.c.   1大匙 = 15 c.c.

1 t. (1 teaspoon) = 5 c.c.   1小匙 = 5 c.c.

Recipe measurements in this book (pp.8 thru 77) are designed for two servings.

本食譜份量爲四人份

Chinese Home Style Stock 中式家常高湯   *Makes 5 cups 5杯*

Heat 1 T. oil. Stir-fry green onion, ginger root and garlic briefly. Add 2 T. small dried fish or shrimp; stir-fry until fragrant. Add 1 T. soy sauce and cook until fragrant; add 5 c. of water. Cook 10 more minutes. Add nappa, cabbage, spinach or tofu if desired.

油1大匙燒熱，將蔥、薑、蒜略炒，再入魚乾或蝦米2大匙炒香，隨入醬油1大匙，香味冒出即加水5杯燒煮約10分鐘，湯內可加白菜、菠菜、豆腐等。

Vegetarian Stock 素高湯   *Makes 5 cups 5杯*

Heat 1 T. oil; stir-fry 5 presoftened Chinese black mushrooms until fragrant. Add 8 cups of water and 2/3 lb. (300g) any combination of vegetables, corn, and soy bean sprouts; cook 30 minutes. Filter liquid to finish stock.

油1大匙燒熱，將香菇5朵(泡軟)炒香，加水8杯及任選蔬菜、玉米、黃豆芽等共8兩(300公克)，煮30分鐘後過濾即成。

4

Chicken (or pork) Stock
鷄(或豬)高湯

Makes 8 cups　8 杯

1　total of 1 ⅓ lb. (600g) chicken bones, chicken wings, chicken legs, whole chicken, or pork bones.

2　2 green onions,
2 slices of ginger root,
3 T. cooking wine,
12 c. of water.

1　Clean ingredients  . Place  and  in a pot.

2　Bring to boil. Reduce heat to medium and remove surface debris.

3　Continue to cook until the soup surface is clear; reduce heat to low and boil uncovered for another 1 to 1 1/2 hours.

4　Cool and filter the liquid to finish stock. Canned chicken broth (contains 3/4 t. salt) may be purchased in supermarkets.

1　鷄骨、鷄翅、鷄腿、全鷄或豬骨‥‥‥‥‥‥任選1斤 (600公克)

2　蔥‥‥‥‥‥2支，薑‥‥‥‥‥2片
酒 ‥‥‥‥‥3大匙，水‥‥‥‥‥12杯

1　將 **1** 料洗淨與 **2** 料放入湯鍋內。

2　大火燒開後，改中火去除泡沫 (燒出來的湯較澄淸)。

3　不再有泡沫浮出時，略降火候 (小滾程度)，不蓋鍋煮約1小時－1 ¹/₂小時。

4　湯冷後過濾即成鷄 (或豬) 高湯。市場有售鷄湯罐頭 (含鹽量約³/₄小匙) 可取代自製高湯。

Ground Meat Stock
絞肉高湯

²/₃ lb. (300g) any combination:
    ground chicken, beef or pork

2 green onions (smashed)
2 slices ginger root
¹/₄ c. each: cooking wine, water

8 c. water

1 Place  in a pot then squeeze out ginger and green onion juice.

2 Add ground pork and mix well.

3 Add 8 c. water then stir to separate ingredients.

4 Bring to boil; reduce heat to medium and remove surface debris. Reduce heat to low and boil 30 minutes. Cool and filter liquid to finish stock. More flavorful stock is produced from ground meat.

雞、牛或豬絞肉任選8兩(300公克)

蔥(拍扁) ………2支，薑……2片
酒、水 ……………………各¹/₄杯

水 ……………………………8杯

1 將  料放入湯鍋內，抓擠至蔥、薑出汁。

2 加入絞肉拌勻。

3 再放入水8杯攪散。

4 大火燒開後，改中火去除泡沫，略降火候(小滾程度)，不蓋鍋煮約30分鐘，待冷過濾即成。此湯是由絞肉燒煮的，容易出味，省時簡便。

Bouillon
西式高湯

1 1 ²/₃ lb. (750g) any combination: beef, chicken bones, chicken legs

2 1 carrot, 1 onion, 1 celery stalk

3 2 cinnamon leaves
¹/₄ c. cooking wine, 12 c. water

1 牛肉、鷄骨或鷄腿…任選1斤4兩
(750公克)

2 紅蘿蔔………1條，洋蔥……1個
西芹 ………………………1支

3 玉桂葉 ………2片，酒……¹/₄杯
水 ………………………12杯

1 Clean ingredient **1** then place in a pot. Add in **2** and **3**.

2 Bring to boil; reduce heat to medium and remove surface debris.

3 Reduce heat to low when all debris is gone. Uncover and boil 1 1/2 hours (boil 2 hours if using beef). Cool, then filter liquid to finish stock.

1 將 **1** 料洗淨，放入湯鍋內，再放入 **2** 、 **3** 料。

2 大火燒開後，改中火去除泡沫(燒出來的湯較澄清)。

3 不再有泡沫浮出時，略降火候(小滾程度)，不蓋鍋煮約1 ¹/₂小時(如使用牛肉時，燒煮時間需加長30分鐘)，待冷過濾即成。

Japanese style stock (see P. 71)
日式高湯 （見71頁）

7

¼ lb.(115g) shelled shrimp

1. ⅛ t. salt
   pinch of pepper
   1 t. cornstarch
   1 t. each: sesame oil, cooking wine

20 won ton skins

2. ¾ t. salt
   pinch of pepper
   1 t. sesame oil
   6 c. stock or water

¼ lb.(115g) leafy vegetables

2 T. chopped green onion

蝦仁	··················	3兩(115公克)

1
鹽	··················	$1/_8$匙
胡椒	··················	少許
太白粉	··················	1小匙
麻油、酒	··················	各1小匙

餛飩皮	··················	20張

2
鹽	··················	$3/_4$小匙
胡椒	··················	少許
麻油	··················	1小匙
高湯或水	··················	6杯

小白菜(切段)	······	3兩(115公克)
蔥花	··················	2大匙

Shrimp Won Ton Soup

蝦仁餛飩湯

1 Mince shrimp then mix with mixture **1** to make filling. Put one portion of filling in center of each skin; fold and seal skin to enclose filling.

2 Bring **2** to boil then add in won tons; bring to another boil then reduce heat to medium and continue cooking 4 minutes or until cooked. Add in vegetables and bring to boil; sprinkle with green onion. Serve.

■ To have clear soup, cook won tons in a separate pot of boiling water.

1 蝦仁剁碎，調入 **1** 料拌勻成餡。每張餛飩皮包入適量的餡，即成餛飩。

2 **2** 料燒開，加入餛飩再燒開，改中火煮4分鐘至熟，續入小白菜再燒開，撒上蔥花即成。

■ 如將餛飩另在滾水內煮熟撈出，放入湯內，做出來的餛飩湯較清。

Pork Won Ton Soup

豬肉餛飩湯

1 Replace shelled shrimp with pork or use one-half shelled shrimp and one-half pork; other ingredients and procedures are the same as "Shrimp Won Ton Soup," above.

1 將蝦仁全部改用豬肉，或蝦仁、豬肉各半，其他材料做法如上。

1. ¹/₆ lb.(75g) ground meat

    ¹/₈ t. salt
    pepper,sesame oil as desired
    1 t. cornstarch
    ¹/₂ T. fried shallots

2. 1 ¹/₄ c. glutinous rice powder
    ¹/₂ c. warm water

    6 sections green onion, 1" (3cm)
        long

3. ¹/₂ t. each: salt, sesame oil
    pinch of pepper
    6 c. stock or water

    ¹/₄ lb.(115g) spinach or other
        leafy vegetable

絞肉	················	2兩(75公克)

①
鹽	··························	⅛小匙
胡椒、麻油	················	各少許
太白粉	······················	1小匙
炸香紅蔥頭	··················	½大匙

②
糯米粉	····················	1¼杯
溫水	························	½杯

蔥(3公分長)	················	6段

③
鹽、麻油	················	各½小匙
胡椒	··························	少許
高湯或水	·····················	6杯

唐好菜或菠菜	······	3兩(115公克)

Rice Ball Soup

鹹湯圓

1 Mix ground meat with **①** thoroughly to make filling; divide into 12 portions.

2 Mix **②** and knead into a smooth rice dough; roll into a long roll and separate into 12 pieces. Shape each dough into a thin circle; place one portion of filling in center of dough. Pinch to seal.

3 Heat 2 T. oil; stir-fry onions until fragrant. Add **③** and bring to boil, then add rice balls. Bring to another boil then reduce heat to medium; cook 5 minutes or until rice balls rise to surface, add vegetables and turn off heat; remove. Dried shrimp, fresh garlic or other ingredients may be added to enhance flavor.

1 將絞肉調入 **①** 料拌勻成餡,分成12等份。

2 **②** 料揉成糯米糰,分成12等份,分別用手捏成圓薄片,再包入餡搓成鹹湯圓。

3 油2大匙燒熱,炒香蔥段,隨入 **③** 料燒開,放入湯圓再燒開,改中火續煮5分鐘或湯圓浮出水面,加唐好菜即可。湯內可依喜好加入蝦米、蒜苗等以增香味。

½ lb.(225g) ground chicken, beef or pork (or minced fish or shrimp)

1.
¼ t. salt
pepper, sesame oil as desired
1 T. each: cornstarch, cooking wine
1 egg white

2.
½ t. salt
pepper, sesame oil as desired
5 c. stock

3.
total of 4 T.(chopped):
coriander or green onion, celery

絞肉(鶏、牛或豬)
或魚、蝦(剁碎)…6兩(225公克)

1	鹽 ……………………¹/₄小匙 胡椒、麻油 ………………各少許 太白粉、酒 …………各1大匙 蛋白 ……………………1個
2	鹽 ……………………¹/₂小匙 胡椒、麻油 ………………各少許 高湯 ……………………5杯
3	香菜或蔥花、芹菜 ……共4大匙

Meat Ball Soup

丸子湯

1   Mix ground meat with **1** until sticky. Squeeze mixture into 16 balls.

2   Bring **2** to boil; add meat balls then bring to boil again. Reduce heat to medium and cook 5 minutes; sprinkle with **3**. Serve.

■   Ready-made meat balls may be used to save time.

1   絞肉調入 **1** 料拌勻至有黏性後，擠成丸子(約16個)。

2   將 **2** 料燒開，加入丸子再燒開，改中火續煮5分鐘，撒上 **3** 料即成。

■   可買現成喜歡的丸子，使用簡便。

¹/₃ lb.(150g) fish fillet

1. pinch of salt
    1 ¹/₂ t. each: cooking wine, cornstarch

    ¹/₃ lb.(150g) spinach or other leafy vegetable

2. ³/₄ t. salt
    1 t. each: cooking wine, sesame oil
    1 T. shredded fresh ginger root
    5 c. stock

¹/₃ lb.(150g) any combination of fish fillet, shelled shrimp, squid, fresh scallops

1 & 2 the same as above recipe

8 slices each: Chinese peapods, carrot

¹/₄ lb.(115g) ready-made crispy rice

14

魚肉 ·············4兩 (150公克)

1
鹽 ···········少許
酒、太白粉 ···········各 1 1/2 小匙

菠菜或西洋菜 ······4兩 (150公克)

2
鹽 ···········3/4 小匙
酒、麻油 ···········各 1 小匙
嫩薑絲 ···········1 大匙
高湯 ···········5 杯

魚肉、蝦仁、魷魚、鮮甘貝
········切片任選共4兩 (150公克)

1 、 **2** 料同上

豌豆莢、紅蘿蔔 ···········各 8 片

鍋粑 ···········3兩 (115公克)
(市面上有售)

Spinach & Fish Soup
菠菜魚片湯

1 Slice the fish meat; add mixture **1** and marinate briefly. Cut spinach into 2" (5cm) long sections.

2 Bring **2** to boil then add spinach. Bring to another boil; add fish slices one by one. Bring to boil again; remove.

1 魚肉切片，調入 **1** 料略醃；菠菜切5公分長段。

2 將 **2** 料燒開，入菠菜再燒開，魚肉一片片放入再燒開即成。

Crispy Rice & Seafood Soup
海鮮鍋粑湯

1 Marinate fish fillet in mixture **1** briefly.

2 Bring **2** to boil. Add marinated fish, Chinese pea pods and carrot, then bring to boil.

3 Heat oil, for deep-frying, fry crispy rice over medium heat 2 minutes until rice expands. Remove and place rice in a bowl then pour into soup. Serve.

1 魚肉等調入 **1** 料略醃。

2 將 **2** 料燒開，入醃好的魚肉、豌豆莢及紅蘿蔔再燒開備用。

3 炸油燒熱，中火將鍋粑炸約2分鐘至漲大，撈出置湯碗內，倒入煮好的湯即成。

15

⅓ lb.(150g) fish fillet

1 T. cooking wine

⅙ lb.(75g) spinach or other leafy
   vegetable

1 c. Chinese fried crueller, cut
   in ½" (1cm) pieces

oil for deep-frying

1 ½ T. ground peanuts or sesame
   seeds (optional)
2 T. chopped green onion
pepper, sesame oil as desired

2 ¾ t. salt
1 ½ T. vinegar
5 c. stock

魚肉	4兩(150公克)
酒	1大匙
豌豆苗或菠菜	2兩(75公克)
油條(切1公分長)	1杯
炸油	適量

1
花生粉或芝麻	½大匙
蔥花	2大匙
胡椒、麻油	各少許

2
鹽	¾小匙
醋	1½大匙
高湯	5杯

Fish and Vegetable Soup

湯泡魚生

1 Slice the fillet in paper thin slices; mix with cooking wine. Deep-fry crueller over medium heat until crispy; remove and set aside.

2 Place spinach in bottom of a bowl. Add fried crueller and **1** . Place fish slices on top; do not overlap. Bring **2** to boil; pour over fish slices. Use chopsticks to mix ingredients well. Serve hot. It will be necessary to cook fish slices in **2** if they are cut too thick.

■ Chinese fried crueller is used to enhance flavor, may omit if not available.

1 魚肉切極薄片,加酒拌勻;油條用中火炸酥備用。

2 湯碗內擺豌豆苗,再入油條及 **1** 料,上面鋪魚片(不要重疊),再將燒開的 **2** 料倒入沖熟,用筷子攪勻,趁熱食用。若魚片太厚,則需在 **2** 料內煮熟。

■ 炸過的油條可增加湯的香味,但不是一定要。

1 large tomato (225g)

2 eggs

1 | $^3/_4$ t. salt
pepper, sesame oil as desired
5 c. stock

$^1/_4$ lb.(115g) green leafy vegetable

1 sheet nori

2 eggs

1 same as 1 of above recipe

1 $^1/_2$ T. chopped green onion

番茄1個	6兩（225公克）
鷄蛋	2個
① 鹽	³/₄小匙
胡椒、麻油	各少許
高湯	5杯
青菜	3兩（115公克）

Tomato and Egg Flower Soup

番茄蛋花湯

1 Cut tomato in pieces; lightly beat eggs for later use.

2 Bring tomato and ① to boil. Cook 3 minutes. Add vegetables and bring to boil again. Slowly add eggs in a thin stream; stir lightly. Serve.

1 番茄切塊；鷄蛋打散備用。

2 番茄加 ① 料燒開煮3分鐘，入青菜再燒開，徐徐倒入蛋液略攪即可。

紫菜	1張
鷄蛋	2個
① 料同上	
蔥花	1 ¹/₂大匙

Nori and Egg Flower Soup

紫菜蛋花湯

1 Tear nori into 2" (5cm) squares; lightly beat eggs for later use.

2 Bring ① to boil. Slowly add eggs in a thin stream; stir lightly. Add nori and green onion; serve.

1 紫菜用手撕成5公分四方，鷄蛋打散備用

2 ① 料燒開，徐徐倒入蛋液略攪，加紫菜及蔥花即成。

1. ¼ lb.(115g) beef

   1 t. each: cooking wine, soy sauce
   1 ½ t. cornstarch

2. ½ lb.(225g) tomato
   4 slices ginger root
   ¾ t. salt
   ⅛ t. pepper
   5 c. water

   2 T. chopped green onion

牛瘦肉	…………………	3兩(115公克)
酒、醬油	…………………	各1小匙
太白粉	…………………	1 ½小匙
番茄1個	…………	6兩(225公克)
薑	…………………………	4片
鹽	…………………………	¾小匙
胡椒	…………………………	⅛小匙
水	…………………………	5杯
蔥花	…………………………	2大匙

1 (for 酒、醬油、太白粉 group)

2 (for 番茄、薑、鹽、胡椒、水 group)

Beef and Tomato Soup

番茄牛肉湯

1 Slice the beef into paper thin slices then briefly marinate in **1**. Slice tomato.

2 Bring **2** to boil. Reduce heat to medium and cook 3 minutes. Add in beef slices one by one. Bring to boil then sprinkle with chopped green onion. Serve.

■ This soup is clear, tasty, and easy to make.

1 牛肉切薄片，調入 **1** 料略醃；番茄切片備用。

2 將 **2** 料燒開，改中火續煮3分鐘，將牛肉一片片放入再燒開，撒上蔥花即可。

■ 此為簡單清爽的湯。

1 lb.(450g) winter melon

¹/₄ lb.(115g) chicken or pork, diced

1 | pinch of salt
1 ¹/₂ t. each: cooking wine, cornstarch

2 | 4 Chinese black mushrooms, presoftened in cold water and diced
2 T. diced ham
1 T. minced ginger root
³/₄ t. salt
pepper, sesame oil as desired
5 c. stock

冬瓜	……………	12兩(450公克)
鷄或豬肉(切丁)	…	3兩(115公克)

1
鹽	……………	少許
酒、太白粉	……	各1½小匙

2
香菇(泡軟、切丁)	…………	4朵
火腿(切丁)	………………	2大匙
薑(切碎)	…………………	1大匙
鹽	………………………	¾小匙
胡椒、麻油	………………	各少許
高湯	……………………	5杯

Winter Melon Soup
冬瓜湯

1   Pare the skin from winter melon and remove the seeds to yield a net weight of 1/2 lb.(225g); dice and mix chicken with **1**.

2   Bring melon and **2** to boil; cook 3 minutes. Add chicken and stir to separate; cook for 2 more minutes. Serve.

■   If Chinese ham is used, reduce the salt in **2**.

■   If Chinese black mushrooms and ham are not available; melon, shredded ginger and stock will also make a delicious soup.

1   冬瓜去皮、籽後約6兩(225公克)，切丁。肉丁調入 **1** 料拌勻。

2   將 **2** 料加冬瓜丁燒開，續煮3分鐘，隨入肉丁拌開，再煮2分鐘即成。

■   如使用中國火腿，因較鹹，故鹽份量可酌量減少。

■   如無香菇及火腿，僅使用冬瓜、薑絲及高湯也可做出一道美味的冬瓜湯。

²/₃ lb. (300g) total of (sliced):
potato (soaked in water),
onion, carrot

1

2 T. butter

³/₄ t. salt
pinch of pepper
5 c. stock

2

1 T. minced coriander

4 strips of bacon or Chinese
salty pork

¹/₄ lb.(115g) celery, cut in
sections

¹/₂ t. salt
pinch of pepper
1 t. sesame oil
5 c. stock

1

洋芋(切片,泡水)、洋蔥、
1 紅蘿蔔(切片) …共8兩(300公克)

奶油 ……………………2大匙

鹽 …………………………³/₄小匙
2 胡椒 …………………………少許
高湯 …………………………5杯

香菜(切碎) ………………1大匙

Potato Soup
洋芋片湯

1 Briefly stir-fry **1** in melted butter. Add **2** ; bring to boil. Reduce heat to medium and cook 5 minutes until potato is tender; sprinkle with coriander. Add clams if desired.

1 奶油略燒熱,待溶化後,先入 **1** 料略炒,續入 **2** 料燒開,改中火煮約5分鐘至洋芋軟,撒上香菜。湯內亦可加入蛤蜊。

培根或肴肉 …………………4片

芹菜(切段) ………3兩(115公克)

鹽 ………¹/₂小匙,胡椒……少許
1 麻油 …………………………1小匙
高湯 …………………………5杯

Bacon and Celery Soup
培根(肴肉)芹菜湯

1 Wrap each bacon strip in a paper towel; cook in microwave at high for 3 minutes to release fat. Remove and cut in strips.

2 Bring **1** to boil. Add bacon and celery; bring to boil again. Reduce heat to medium and cook 2 more minutes. Serve.

1 培根一片片用紙巾包住,用微波爐高溫煮3分鐘(去除油質),取出切條狀。

2 將 **1** 料燒開,入培根及芹菜再燒開,改中火續煮2分鐘即成。

25

¼ lb.(115g) boneless chicken breast, sliced

1. pinch of salt
   1 ½ t. each: cooking wine, cornstarch

4 eggs

2. ½ T. soy sauce
   1 T. cooking wine

3. ½ t. salt
   pinch of pepper
   5 c. stock

1 c. broccoli or nappa cabbage

鷄胸肉（切薄片）…3兩（115公克）

1 鹽 ……………………………………少許
酒、太白粉 …………各1½小匙

鷄蛋 ……………………………4個

2 醬油 ……………………………½大匙
酒 ………………………………1大匙

3 鹽 ……………………………………½小匙
胡椒 ……………………………少許
高湯 ……………………………5杯

靑花菜或白菜 ………………1杯

Chicken Slices and Egg Soup

鷄片荷包蛋湯

1 Mix chicken slices with **1**; cut broccoli in small pieces.

2 Heat 2 T. oil. Fry each egg until both sides are golden; add **2** and cook until fragrant. Add **3**; bring to boil. Add vegetables, then chicken slices one by one; bring to another boil. Serve.

1 肉片調入 **1** 料；靑花菜切小朵備用。

2 油2大匙燒熱，將每個鷄蛋煎成荷包蛋，加 **2** 料略煮至香味溢出，再加 **3** 料燒開後，隨入蔬菜及鷄肉一片一片放入燒開即成。

1. ¼ lb.(115g) chicken, beef or pork, sliced

    1 t. each: cooking wine, soy sauce
    1 ½ t. cornstarch

    5 c. stock

    1 ¾ oz.(50g) bean threads

2. 8 slices of each: pickled mustard greens , gherkin cucumber
    ⅔ T. each: chopped green onion, soy sauce
    pepper, sesame oil as desired

    ½ t. salt

鷄、牛或豬肉(切片) ………3兩
(115公克)

1　酒、醬油 ………………各1小匙
　　太白粉 …………………1 1/2小匙

高湯 …………………………5杯

乾粉絲1小把 ……1.5兩(50公克)

2　榨菜、小黃瓜 ……………各8片
　　葱花、醬油 ……………各2/3大匙
　　胡椒、麻油 ………………各少許

鹽 …………………………1/2小匙

Bean Thread and Cucumber Soup

黃瓜細粉湯

1　Mix meat with ❶. Soak bean threads in water until soft (yielding about 1 c.). Cut bean threads as desired. Soak mustard greens in water for 2 minutes.

2　Bring stock to boil; add bean threads; bring to boil. Add chicken slices one by one, bring to boil again. Add ❷ and turn off heat immediately *. Test saltiness then add salt as needed. Serve.

■　The purpose of turning off heat immediately after adding mustard greens and cucumber is to preserve their crispiness.

1　肉片調入 ❶ 料備用；粉絲用水泡軟，略切(約1杯)。榨菜片洗淨泡水2分鐘備用。

2　將高湯燒開，放入粉絲再燒開，將肉一片片放入再燒開，最後加 ❷ 料熄火，試鹹淡再加鹽即成。

■　榨菜及小黃瓜放入湯內後便立即熄火，保持其脆度。

²/₃ lb.(300g) clams

1

1 T. shredded ginger root
pinch of salt
1 T. cooking wine
5 c. stock or water

蛤蜊 ·················8兩（300公克）

① 薑絲 ··························1大匙
鹽 ······························少許
酒 ······························1大匙
高湯或水 ·····················5杯

Clam Soup

蛤蜊湯

1   Rinse clams or briefly soak clams in salt solution (1 1/2 c. water and 1 t. salt) to release sand.

2   Bring ① to boil; add clams and boil for another minute. Remove surface debris.

■   If more clams and ginger root are added, plain water may be used for stock.

1   蛤蜊洗淨或用鹽水（1 ½杯水加1小匙鹽）略泡吐沙。

2   將 ① 料燒開，入蛤蜊再燒開煮1分鐘，去除泡沫即成。

■   蛤蜊本身味很鮮，多加蛤蜊及薑，不用高湯也可以。

1/4 c. shredded Chinese black mushrooms, presoftened in cold water

1 | 1/4 c. each (shredded): bamboo shoots, ham
1 c. shredded white pressed bean curd

pepper, sesame oil as desired

2 | 1 T. cooking wine
5 c. stock

3/4 t. salt

1 lb.(450g) fish

3 T. lard or cooking oil

6 sections green onion, 1"(3cm)

6 slices ginger root

1 | 1 T. cooking wine
2 c. shredded white radish
6 c. water

3/4 t. salt

2 | pinch of pepper
4 T. milk

香菇（泡軟，切絲）…………¼杯
1 筍、火腿（切絲）…………各¼杯
白豆乾（切絲）……………1杯

胡椒、麻油 ……………各少許
2 酒 ……………………………1大匙
高湯 ……………………………5杯

鹽 …………………………¾小匙

魚 ……………12兩（450公克）

豬油或沙拉油 ……………3大匙

蔥…………6段，薑…………6片

1 蘿蔔絲 ……………………………2杯
酒…………1大匙，水………6杯

2 鹽 ………¾小匙，胡椒……少許
牛奶 ……………………………4大匙

Three-flavored Soup
三鮮干絲湯

1 Bring **2** to boil. Add **1**; boil again. Reduce heat to medium; cook 5 more minutes then add salt.

1 將 **2** 料燒開，放入 **1** 料再燒開，改中火續煮5分鐘再加鹽即可。

Fish and White Radish Soup
蘿蔔絲魚湯

1 Clean fish (gold carp, grouper or scup), pat dry.

2 Heat lard. Fry fish until both sides are golden brown; move fish to side of wok. Stir-fry green onion and ginger root until fragrant. Add **1** and cook 15 minutes over high heat; add **2**. Remove fish. Sprinkle soy sauce, vinegar and sesame oil on fish. Serve soup and fish separately.

1 魚（鯽魚、石斑魚或鯛魚）處理乾淨，拭乾水份備用。

2 豬油燒熱，大火將魚煎至兩面呈金黃色後鏟至鍋邊，隨入蔥、薑炒香，續入 **1** 料大火燒煮15分鐘，再加 **2** 料即成。食時將魚撈出置盤，淋上醬油、醋及麻油即成另一道菜餚。

¼ lb.(115g) chicken, beef or pork

1
1 t. each: soy sauce, cooking
    wine
1½ t. cornstarch

2
5 c. stock
⅓ c. shredded bamboo shoots
⅓ c. shredded Chinese black
    mushrooms*

3
⅓ c. pickled mustard greens,
    shredded
1 T. chopped green onion
pepper, sesame oil as desired
⅔ T. soy sauce

⅓ t. salt

鷄、牛或豬肉	……3兩(115公克)	

1	醬油、酒 …………………各1小匙	
	太白粉 …………………1 ½小匙	

2	高湯 ……………………5杯	
	筍絲 ……………………⅓杯	
	香菇(泡軟、切絲) …………⅓杯	

3	榨菜 ……………………⅓杯	
	蔥花 ……………………1大匙	
	胡椒、麻油 ………………各少許	
	醬油 ……………………⅔大匙	

鹽 ………………………⅓小匙		

Mustard Greens and Pork Shred Soup

榨菜肉絲湯

1 Shred the meat; mix with **1**

2 Soak mustard greens in water 2 minutes; remove and squeeze out water.

3 Bring **2** to boil; add shredded meat. Stir lightly to separate the shreds; bring to boil again. Add **3** ; then taste for saltiness. Add salt as needed.

■ Different brands of pickled mustard greens vary in saltiness. Test for saltiness before adding salt.

* Chinese black mushrooms should be soaked in cold water until soft before shredding.

1 肉切絲，調入 **1** 料備用。

2 榨菜切絲，泡水 2 分鐘，擠乾水份備用。

3 將 **2** 料燒開，加入肉絲攪散再燒開，放入 **3** 料試鹹淡後再加鹽即可。

■ 榨菜因廠牌不同，鹹淡亦不同，加鹽時注意。

½ chicken, 1 ⅓ lbs. (600g)

8 small Chinese black mush-
    rooms, presoftened in cold
    water

1 | ¾ t. salt
1 T. cooking wine
5 c. water

鷄半隻 ·············	1斤 (600公克)
小香菇 (泡軟) ·················	8朶
1 鹽 ·····························	3/4小匙
酒 ·····························	1大匙
水 ·····························	5杯

Chicken & Chinese Black Mushrooms

香菇燉鷄湯

1   Clean then cut chicken in pieces; blanch in boiling water. Stew chicken pieces and **1** in a casserole over high heat for 40 minutes. (If a pot is used, add 2 more cups of water, bring to boil, cover and cook over low heat 30 minutes.) Add mushrooms; continue stewing 15 more minutes.

1   鷄洗淨切塊，用滾水川燙後，加 **1** 料放入燉鍋內燉40分鐘 (若用湯鍋，則多加2杯水，燒開後改小火蓋鍋煮30分鐘) 再加香菇續燉或煮15分鐘即成。

1. 2 lbs.(900g) winter melon
   1 large chicken leg
   8 slices ham
   4 Chinese black mushrooms,
     presoftened in cold water
   2 dried scallops

2. 2 slices ginger root
   1 T. cooking wine
   5 c. stock or water

   ³/₄ t. salt

	冬瓜 ················24兩(900公克)	
	鷄腿(大) ······················1隻	
1	火腿 ·······························8片	
	香菇(泡軟) ····················4朵	
	乾干貝 ·························2個	
	薑 ·······························2片	
2	酒 ····························1大匙	
	高湯或水 ······················5杯	
	鹽 ·······························3/4小匙	

Stewed Winter Melon Soup

原盅三味

1 Pare winter melon and remove seeds. Scoop out balls, or make bite-size cubes (to equal about 1 lb., 450g). Cut chicken legs in pieces then blanch in boiling water; remove, drain and discard water. Soak the dried scallops in hot water for 1 hour; remove and drain (shred if desired).

2 Stew **1** and **2** in a casserole over high heat 40 minutes. (If a pot is used, add 2 more cups of water, bring to boil, cover and cook over low heat 30 minutes.) Add salt (ham is salty, use salt with care). Serve.

1 冬瓜去皮、籽，切圓形或方塊狀後約12兩(450公克)，鷄腿切塊，用滾水川燙撈出，干貝泡熱水1小時(可撕成絲)備用。

2 將 **1** 料及 **2** 料放入燉鍋內燉40分鐘，(若用湯鍋，則多加2杯水，燒開後改小火蓋鍋煮30分鐘)再加鹽即成。火腿鹹淡不同，鹽可酌量減少。

1 lb.(450g) lotus root

1 large chicken leg

½ c. shelled raw peanuts*

① 2 T. cooking wine
8 c. stock or water

¾ t. salt

蓮藕	12兩 (450公克)
鷄腿 (大)	1隻
生花生 (去皮的) *	½杯

①	
酒	2大匙
高湯或水	8杯

鹽	¾小匙

Lotus Root and Peanut Soup

蓮藕花生湯

1 Soak peanuts for 1 hour in 4 c. boiled hot water; remove and drain. Cut off both ends of lotus root then pare skin, yielding 1/2 lb. (225g); slice in 1/4" (0.5cm) thickness. Cut chicken leg in pieces.

2 Add peanuts, chicken pieces and lotus root to ① ; bring to boil. Reduce heat to medium; remove surface debris and cook 40 more minutes, then add salt. Serve.

★ Available in Chinese supermarkets.

1 花生用滾水4杯浸泡1小時後瀝乾，蓮藕去兩端削皮後約6兩 (225公克)，切0.5公分厚片；鷄腿切塊。

2 將花生、鷄腿、蓮藕放入 ① 料內燒開，改中火，去除泡沫，續煮40分鐘加鹽即成。

★ 去皮的生花生中國市場有售。

½ chicken, 1 ⅓ lbs.(600g)

2 T. black sesame oil

4 slices ginger root

2 ½ c. rice cooking wine

½ duck, 1 ⅓ lbs. (600g)

1 4 slices each: tang kuei, ginger root
½ c. cooking wine
5 c. water

¾ t. salt

鷄半隻	1斤(600公克)
黑麻油	2大匙
薑	4片
米酒	2 1/2杯

Sesame Oil and Chicken Soup

麻油鷄湯

1 Cut chicken in pieces.

2 Heat wok then add sesame oil. Stir-fry ginger root over medium heat until fragrant and golden; add chicken pieces and stir-fry over high heat 3 minutes. Add cooking wine and bring to boil. Add 2 1/2 c. water; bring to boil again. Reduce heat to medium and cook 30 more minutes.

■ This soup is popular and is an excellent nutrient for women who have recently given birth and need to regain their strength quickly. To enhance the flavor of the soup, replace the water with rice cooking wine.

1 鷄切塊備用。

2 黑麻油2大匙燒熱，用中火炒香薑片至金黃色，隨入鷄塊大火煎爆3分鐘，加酒燒開入水2 1/2杯再燒開，改中火煮30分鐘即成。

■ 此道菜若全部用酒來燒煮不加水味更香濃，是為婦女生產後的最佳補品。

Dang Kuei and Duck Soup

當歸鴨湯

鴨半隻	1斤(600公克)
當歸、薑	各4片
1 酒	1/2杯
水	5杯
鹽	3/4小匙

1 Cut duck in pieces then blanch in boiling water. Remove and transfer to a casserole. Add in [1] and stew 1 hour until meat is tender. (If a pot is used, add 2 additional cups of water, bring to boil, cover and cook over low heat for 1 hour). Add salt and serve.

1 鴨洗淨切塊，用滾水川燙後，加 [1] 料放入燉鍋內燉約1小時至鴨肉熟軟(若用湯鍋，則多加2杯水，燒開後改小火蓋鍋煮約1小時)，再加鹽即成。

1 ⅓ lbs.(600g) beef shank or oxtails

1. total of 2 ⅔ lbs.(1200g): onions, tomatoes, carrots, potatoes and cabbage (cut in pieces)

2. 1 t. salt
   1 T. each: soy sauce, cooking wine

牛腱或牛尾 ⋯⋯⋯1斤 (600公克)

1 洋蔥、番茄、紅蘿蔔、馬鈴薯
包心菜 ⋯切塊共2斤 (1200公克)

2 鹽 ⋯⋯⋯⋯⋯⋯⋯⋯⋯⋯⋯1小匙
醬油、酒 ⋯⋯⋯⋯⋯各1大匙

Lo Sung Beef Soup

羅宋湯

1 Cut beef in pieces. Add 12 cups of water and bring to boil; turn heat to medium; remove surface debris and cook 1 hour. Add **1**; boil again over high heat. Reduce heat to medium and cook 40 minutes. Add ingredient **2** for flavor. Serve.

1 牛腱切塊，加水12杯燒開，改中火，去除泡沫，煮約1小時，加 **1** 料大火再燒開，改中火續煮40分鐘，加 **2** 料調味即成。

½ lb.(225g) spare ribs, cut in pieces

1 tomato

½ lb.(225g) soybean sprouts

1 | 2 slices of ginger root
7 c. water

¾ t. salt

46

小排骨 (切塊) ……6兩 (225公克)

番茄 …………………………1個

黃豆芽 …………6兩 (225公克)

1 | 薑 …………………………2片
水 …………………………7杯

鹽 ……………………³/₄小匙

Bean Sprouts and Spare Ribs Soup

排骨豆芽湯

1 Lightly score crisscross on non-stem end of tomato. Blanch tomato in boiling water; remove. Remove skin, then seeds. Cut the tomato in pieces.

2 Add spare ribs to ❶; bring to boil. Remove surface debris; reduce heat to medium and cook 20 minutes. Add tomatoes, bean sprouts and salt; bring to boil over high heat. Reduce heat to medium and cook 20 minutes. Serve.

1 在番茄頂端劃十字刀痕，放入滾水內川燙撈出，去皮、去籽後切塊。

2 將排骨放入 ❶ 料內燒開，改中火，去除泡沫煮20分鐘，加番茄、黃豆芽及鹽大火再燒開，改中火續煮20分鐘即可。

1 lb.(450g) beef shanks

1 1 red chili, cut in sections
6 slices ginger root
4 T. cooking wine
8 c. water

2 $^3/_4$ t. salt
$^1/_4$ t. pepper
1 t. chopped green onion
2 T. coriander

48

牛腱	··············	12兩(450公克)

	紅辣椒 (切段)	················1支
1	薑	················6片
	酒	················4大匙
	水	················8杯

	鹽	················$^3/_4$小匙
2	胡椒	················$^1/_4$小匙
	蔥花	················1小匙
	香菜	················2大匙

Peppered Beef Soup

椒麻牛肉湯

1 Cut beef shank in 1/2" (1.5cm) thick slices then place in **1** ; bring to boil. Remove surface debris; reduce heat to medium and cook 1 to 1 1/2 hours or until meat is tender. Add **2** . Serve.

■ Add 1/2 t. Szechuan Peppercorns to **1** for extra flavor.

1 牛腱切1.5公分厚片，放入 **1** 料內燒開，去除．　　　改中火煮約1 — 1$^1/_2$小時，至牛肉軟，加 **2** 料即成。

■ 如喜歡花椒的香味，可在 **1** 料內加花椒粒 $^1/_2$ 小匙

1
- 1 c. cleaned pig tripe, precooked and cut in strips*
- ½ c. pickled mustard cabbage, cut in strips
- ⅓ c. shredded bamboo shoots
- total of 5 c.: stock and retained broth from cooking pig tripe

2
- salt as desired
- 1 t. sesame oil
- 1 T. shredded ginger root (optional)

熟豬肚(切條)*	·················	1杯
酸菜(切條)	·················	½杯
筍絲	·················	⅓杯
高湯加煮豬肚湯	············	共5杯

(1)

鹽	·················	適量
麻油	·················	1小匙
薑絲(無亦可)	·············	1大匙

(2)

Tripe With Mustard Cabbage Soup

酸菜豬肚湯

1 Bring ① to boil; reduce heat to medium and cook 5 minutes. Test for saltiness then add ②. Serve.

★ **TO COOK PIG TRIPE:** Add 2 green onions , 2 slices of ginger root, 1 T. cooking wine, and tripe to 6 c. water. Bring to boil; reduce heat to medium and cook 40 minutes. Remove and cut tripe in strips.

1 將 ① 料燒開，改中火續煮5分鐘，試鹹淡再加 ② 料即成。

★ **豬肚處理法**

1 豬肚除去污油，以鹽、醋搓揉至無黏液時，沖洗乾淨，放入滾水內煮3分鐘撈出，刮下白垢再洗淨(可買現成乾淨豬肚)。

2 將水6杯、蔥2枝、薑2片、酒1大匙連同乾淨豬肚燒開，改中火煮約40分鐘，取出切條即可煮湯或做其他用途。

½ lb. (225g) tofu, shredded

½ c. shredded pork, beef or chicken

1 | 1 t. each: cooking wine, soy sauce
1 t. cornstarch

2 | ¾ t. salt
5 c. stock

3 | 3 T. cornstarch
4 T. water

2 eggs, beaten

4 | 2 T. each: soy sauce, vinegar
⅓ t. each: pepper, sesame oil
1 T. each (shredded): green onion, ginger root
1 T. minced coriander

豆腐 (切絲) ⋯⋯⋯6兩 (225公克)

肉絲 (豬、牛或鷄) ⋯⋯⋯⋯¹/₂杯

1
酒、醬油 ⋯⋯⋯⋯⋯⋯各1小匙
太白粉 ⋯⋯⋯⋯⋯⋯⋯⋯1小匙

2
鹽 ⋯⋯⋯⋯⋯⋯⋯⋯⋯⋯³/₄小匙
高湯 ⋯⋯⋯⋯⋯⋯⋯⋯⋯5杯

3
太白粉 ⋯⋯⋯⋯⋯⋯⋯⋯3大匙
水 ⋯⋯⋯⋯⋯⋯⋯⋯⋯4大匙

鷄蛋 (打散) ⋯⋯⋯⋯⋯⋯2個

4
醬油、醋 ⋯⋯⋯⋯⋯⋯各2大匙
胡椒、麻油 ⋯⋯⋯⋯各¹/₃小匙
蔥絲、薑絲 ⋯⋯⋯⋯各1大匙
香菜 (切碎) ⋯⋯⋯⋯⋯1大匙

Hot and Sour Soup

酸辣湯

1 Briefly marinate meat with **1**.

2 Bring **2** to boil; add meat and stir to separate. Add tofu; bring to boil. Add mixture **3**; stir to thicken. Slowly add eggs in a thin stream; stir lightly then turn off heat immediately. Add **4**; mix and serve.

■ Add shredded Chinese black mushrooms, carrots and wood ears as desired.

1 肉絲調入 **1** 料略醃。

2 將 **2** 料燒開,肉絲放入湯內攪散,續加豆腐燒開,再以調勻的 **3** 料勾成薄汁後徐徐淋入蛋汁略攪動使其散開,立即熄火,放入 **4** 料即成。

■ 亦可在湯內隨意加入紅蘿蔔、香菇、木耳等材料。

Tofu Soup

豆腐羹

1 Replace shredded meat with ground meat and **4** with 1 T. soy sauce. Other ingredients and procedures are the same as in "Hot and Sour Soup", above.

1 將肉絲改用絞肉, **4** 料改用醬油1大匙,其他做法同上。

¼ lb.(115g) lean pork, sliced

1
½ T. each: soy sauce, cornstarch
1 T. fried shallots

¼ lb.(115g) fish paste*

2
¼ c. Chinese black mushrooms
   (presoftened in cold water)
½ c. shredded bamboo shoots
¾ t. each: salt, sugar
6 c. water

3
4 T. cornstarch
5 T. water

4
1 T. soy sauce
2 t. black vinegar
sesame oil, pepper, coriander as
   desired

Pork and Fish Paste Soup

肉羹

瘦豬肉(切片) ……3兩(115公克)

1
醬油、太白粉 …………各¹/₂大匙
炸香紅蔥頭 ………………1大匙

魚漿* ……………3兩(115公克)
(可買現成的)

2
泡軟的香菇絲 ………………¹/₄杯
筍絲 ………………………¹/₂杯
鹽、糖 ………………各³/₄小匙
水 …………………………6杯

3
太白粉 ……………………4大匙
水 …………………………5大匙

4
醬油 ………………………1大匙
黑醋 ………………………2小匙
胡椒、麻油、香菜 ………各少許

1 Mix pork slices with ①. Add fish paste and mix thoroughly.

2 Bring ② to boil. Add coated pork slices, one by one; bring to boil. Add mixture ③; stir to thicken. Turn off heat and add ④. Serve.

★ To make fish paste: Clean 1/2 lb.(225g) fillet of fish and mince finely. Add 1/4 t. salt, 1 egg white and 1 T. cornstarch; stir until sticky. Ready-made fish paste is available in Chinese supermarkets.

1 將肉片調入 ① 料,再加魚漿攪勻。

2 ② 料燒開,將裹上魚漿的肉一片片放入湯內燒開,再以調勻的 ③ 料勾成薄汁,熄火,加 ④ 料即成。

★ 魚漿做法:將魚肉6兩(225公克)剁爛,加鹽¹/₄小匙,蛋白1個,太白粉1大匙攪拌至有黏性即成。

½ lb.(225g) fresh squid

1. | ⅛ t. salt
   | 1 T. cooking wine

2. | 6 sections green onion, 1" (3cm) long
   | 1 T. shredded ginger root
   | 1 chili, sliced

3. | ½ lb.(225g) white radish, sliced
   | ½ t. salt
   | 1 t. sugar
   | 5 c. stock

4. | 3 T. cornstarch
   | 4 T. water

5. | 2 T. barbecue (Sa Tsa) sauce
   | 1 T. soy sauce
   | ½ t. black vinegar or vinegar
   | 1 T. minced coriander or onion

新鮮魷魚	··········	6兩(225公克)

1	鹽	··········	¹/₈小匙
	酒	··········	1大匙

2	蔥(3公分長)	··········	6段
	薑絲	··········	1大匙
	辣椒(切片)	··········	1條

3	白蘿蔔(切片)	·····	6兩(225公克)
	鹽	··········	¹/₂小匙
	糖	··········	1小匙
	高湯	··········	5杯

4	太白粉	··········	3大匙
	水	··········	4大匙

5	沙茶醬	··········	2大匙
	醬油	··········	1大匙
	黑醋或醋	··········	¹/₂小匙
	香菜或蔥末	··········	1大匙

Barbecued Squid Soup

沙茶魷魚羹

1. Score crisscross patterns on squid then cut in pieces. Mix with **1** and marinate briefly.

2. Heat 2 T. oil. Stir-fry **2** until fragrant; add squid. Stir-fry 1 minute. Remove and set aside.

3. Bring **3** to boil then cook 5 minutes. Add the squid pieces; boil again. Add mixture **4**; stir to thicken. Add **5**. Serve.

1. 魷魚切花片,調入 **1** 料略醃。

2. 油2大匙燒熱,炒香 **2** 料,並入魷魚炒1分鐘,鏟出備用。

3. 將 **3** 料燒開煮5分鐘,隨入炒好的魷魚再燒開,並以調勻的 **4** 料勾成薄汁,最後加入 **5** 料即成。

¹/₃ **lb.(150g) diced fish fillet**

1
³/₄ **c. soft tofu, cut in small pieces**
¹/₂ **c. sliced mushrooms**
¹/₄ **c. each: ham (cut in small**
    pieces), green peas

2
³/₄ **t. salt**
pepper, sesame oil, cooking
    wine as desired
5 c. stock

3
3 T. cornstarch
4 T. water

4
1 T. water
1 egg white

魚肉(切丁) ……… 4兩(150公克)

1
嫩豆腐(切小片) ……………³/₄杯
洋菇(切小片) ………………¹/₂杯
火腿(切小片)、青豆仁 …各¹/₄杯

2
鹽 ……………………………³/₄小匙
胡椒、麻油、酒 …………各少許
高湯 ……………………………5杯

3
太白粉 ……………………3大匙
水 ……………………………4大匙

4
水 ……………………………1大匙
蛋白 ……………………………1個

Fish Soup

魚羹

1   Bring ② to boil; add ① . Add fish and stir lightly to separate. Bring to boil, add mixture ③ ; stir to thicken. Slowly add ④ ; stir lightly and turn off heat. Serve.

1   將 ② 料燒開，放入 ① 料，再入魚肉輕輕攪開，燒開後加調勻的 ③ 料勾成薄汁 徐徐倒入拌勻的 ④ 料略攪動使其散開，立即熄火。

1. ½ c. crab meat
   ½ c. asparagus, cut 1" (3cm) long
   ½ c. sliced mushrooms
   ¼ c. lima beans or green peas

2. ¾ t. salt
   5 c. stock

3. 3 T. cornstarch
   4 T. water

4. 1 T. water
   1 egg white

60

1	蟹肉	……………………¹/₂杯
	蘆筍(切3公分長)	…………¹/₂杯
	毛菇(切片)	……………………¹/₂杯
	蠶豆或青豆仁	………………¹/₄杯
2	鹽	…………………………³/₄小匙
	高湯	……………………………5杯
3	太白粉	……………………3大匙
	水	…………………………4大匙
4	水	…………………………1大匙
	蛋白	…………………………1個

蟹肉蘆筍湯

1 Bring **2** to boil; add **1** then boil again. Add mixture **3** ; stir to thicken. Slowly add mixture **4** ; stir lightly and turn off heat. Serve.

1 將 **2** 料燒開，隨入 **1** 料再燒開，以調勻的 **3** 料勾成薄汁，徐徐倒入拌勻的 **4** 料略攪動使其散開，立即熄火。

1 | 1 lb. (450g) green peas
2 c. stock

2 | 2 T. butter
2 T. flour

3 | 3/4 t. salt
1/4 t. pepper
2 c. stock

1/2 c. milk

62

1	青豆仁	⋯⋯⋯⋯12兩(450公克)
	高湯	⋯⋯⋯⋯⋯⋯2杯
2	奶油	⋯⋯⋯⋯⋯2大匙
	麵粉	⋯⋯⋯⋯⋯2大匙
3	鹽	⋯⋯⋯⋯⋯³/₄小匙
	胡椒	⋯⋯⋯⋯⋯¹/₄小匙
	高湯	⋯⋯⋯⋯⋯2杯
	鮮奶	⋯⋯⋯⋯⋯¹/₂杯

Green Pea Cream Soup

青豆濃湯

1 Stir-fry **2** over low heat 5 minutes until fragrant and pasty.

2 Bring **1** to boil; cook until green peas are soft then liquify with a blender. Gradually pour small portion of liquified peas over the paste several times and stir until mixed well. Add in **3** ; bring to boil. Add in milk; turn off heat immediately.

1 先用小火將 **2** 料炒香成白糊醬 (約5分鐘)。

2 **1** 料燒開,待青豆仁煮軟後,用果汁機攪爛分次放入白糊醬內攪勻,完全拌勻後,倒入 **3** 料燒開,再加鮮奶立即熄火。

Tomato Cream Soup

番茄濃湯

1 Replace **1** with 3/4 lb. (340g) diced tomato, 1/4 lb. (115g) diced onions, 2 c. stock. Other ingredients and procedures are the same as above. Pumpkin, broccoli, other vegetables, or rice may be used with these procedures to make other cream soups.

1 將 **1** 料改用番茄丁9兩(340公克)、洋蔥丁3兩(115公克)、高湯2杯,其他材料與做法同上,南瓜、西芥蘭或其他蔬菜飯等均可參照上法做。

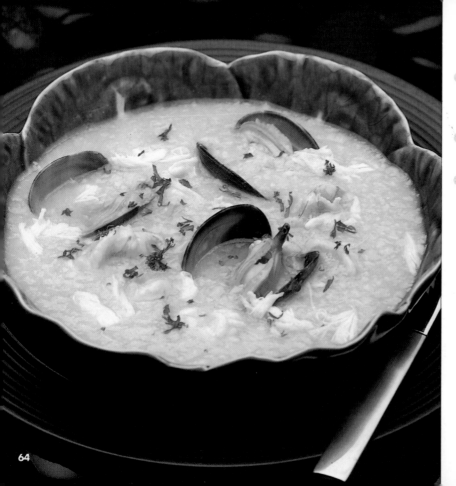

① 1 can corn (about 1 lb.) (450g)
4 c. stock or water
1 T. cooking wine
¾ t. salt
pinch of pepper

② ½ c. any combination: shelled shrimp, crab meat, fish meat, scallops, clams

③ 2 ½ T. cornstarch
3 T. water

1 beaten egg

	玉米罐頭1罐⋯⋯12兩(450公克)
	高湯或水 ⋯⋯⋯⋯⋯⋯⋯⋯⋯4杯
1	酒 ⋯⋯⋯⋯⋯⋯⋯⋯⋯⋯⋯1大匙
	鹽 ⋯⋯⋯⋯⋯⋯⋯⋯⋯³/₄小匙
	胡椒 ⋯⋯⋯⋯⋯⋯⋯⋯⋯⋯少許
2	蝦仁、蟹肉、魚肉
	貝類 ⋯⋯⋯⋯⋯⋯⋯⋯任選¹/₂杯
3	太白粉 ⋯⋯⋯⋯⋯⋯⋯2¹/₂大匙
	水 ⋯⋯⋯⋯⋯⋯⋯⋯⋯⋯⋯3大匙
	蛋(打散) ⋯⋯⋯⋯⋯⋯⋯⋯1個

Corn With Seafood Soup

海鮮玉米羹

1 Bring ❶ to boil; add ❷, boil again. Add mixture ❸ to thicken. Slowly pour egg in a thin stream; stir lightly and turn off heat. Serve.

■ There are two types of canned corn: whole kernel and cream style which can be mixed or used separately.

1 將 ❶ 料燒開，加入 ❷ 料再燒開，以調勻的 ❸ 料勾成薄汁，徐徐倒入蛋液略攪動使其散開，立即熄火。

■ 玉米罐頭有顆粒狀和糊狀二種，可單獨或混合使用。

1. 2 c. nappa cabbage (cut in pieces)
   $\frac{1}{2}$ c. bean threads, presoftened in water
   $\frac{1}{2}$ c. mushrooms

2. 8 slices of each: ham, bamboo shoots, cooked pig tripe*
   8 slices of each: cooked chicken meat or pork, fish cake
   8 slices carrot
   4 Chinese black mushrooms, presoftened in cold water, cut in half

   $\frac{1}{4}$ lb.(115g) fish paste

   12 green peas

3. 1 t. salt
   pinch of pepper
   1 t. sesame oil
   1 T. cooking wine
   5 c. stock

①	大白菜 (切塊)	2杯
	粉絲 (泡軟)	½杯
	洋菇	½杯
②	火腿、筍、熟豬肚＊	各8片
	熟雞肉、魚糕	各8片
	紅蘿蔔	8片
	香菇 (泡軟、切半)	4朵
	魚漿	3兩 (115公克)
	靑豆仁	12粒
③	鹽	1小匙
	胡椒	少許
	麻油	1小匙
	酒	1大匙
	高湯	5杯

Chinese Hot Pot (Huo Kuo)

什錦火鍋

1 Place ① in a casserole; surround with ②. Slice fish paste in long strips; place the slices in casserole and top with green peas (or use 8 fish balls for fish paste and green peas). Add ③ and cover; bring to boil. This is a Chinese style cook-at-table dish, (Fondue Style). Continue to cook while serving and eating.

■ A variety of seafood may be used in ②. Tomato, pickled mustard cabbage or mustard greens may be added to soup to enhance flavor.

★ To cook tripe, see p.51

1 先將 ① 料鋪在火鍋底，② 料排在周圍，再將魚漿刮成長條狀，上置靑豆仁 (或用魚丸8個取代)，最後加 ③ 料蓋鍋，燒開後即可邊煮邊食。

■ ② 料內的材料可依喜好選用不同種類的海鮮，湯內也可加番茄、鹹酸菜或榨菜來增加湯的鮮度。

★ 豬肚處理法見第51頁。

1 ⅓ lb.(600g) fish

1 T. soy sauce

1 fresh garlic clove or green onion

①
8 paper-thin slices lean meat
4 Chinese black mushrooms, presoftened in cold water, cut in half
2 c. nappa cabbage, cut in pieces

⅓ lb.(150g) tofu, cut in pieces

②
¾ t. salt
1 T. each: cooking wine, soy sauce
5 c. stock

魚	·············	1斤 (600公克)
醬油	················	1大匙
蒜苗或蔥	··········	1支

1
瘦肉	·················	8片
香菇 (泡軟、切半)	········	4朵
大白菜 (切塊)	········	2杯

豆腐 (切塊)	······	4兩 (150公克)

2
鹽	·················	3/4小匙
酒、醬油	············	各1大匙
高湯	················	5杯

Stewed Fish Casserole

砂鍋魚

1   Clean fish and pat dry; rub with soy sauce. Cut garlic into pieces; separate white and green parts.

2   Heat 4 T. oil; fry fish 4 minutes, or until both sides are golden brown. Remove.

3   Stir-fry white part of fresh garlic until fragrant. Add **1**; stir-fry briefly. Remove, place in casserole. Add fish, **2** and Tofu; bring to boil. Turn heat to medium and cook 30 minutes. Sprinkle with green garlic pieces and serve. Add bok choy, bean threads, bamboo shoots or carrot if desired.

1   魚處理乾淨，拭乾水份，抹上醬油；蒜苗切段，分蒜白及蒜葉。

2   油4大匙燒熱，將魚煎約4分鐘，至兩面呈金黃色撈出。

3   餘油炒香蒜白，依序入 **1** 料略炒取出，置砂鍋內，再入魚、**2** 料及豆腐燒開，改中火燒煮30分鐘，撒上蒜葉即成。湯內可加入青梗菜、粉絲、筍或紅蘿蔔。

5 c. Japanese style stock

1 | ⅓ lb.(150g) diced soft tofu
½ c. presoftened, sectioned seaweed

2 | 3 T. miso
3 T. water

1 T. chopped green onion

日式高湯 ·····················5杯

1
嫩豆腐 (切小丁) ···4兩 (150公克)
嫩海帶 (泡軟、切段) ········¹/₂杯

2
味噌 ·····················3大匙
水 ·······················3大匙

蔥花 ·····················1大匙

Miso Soup
味噌湯

1 Bring stock to boil. Add ¹ and mixture ² ; boil again. Sprinkle on green onion.

■ Other desired vegetables or seafood may be used for ¹ .

■ **JAPANESE STYLE STOCK:** Soak 2 slices of dried seaweed, 4" (10cm) long, in 8 c. of water for 2-3 hours; remove seaweed (Fig. 1). Bring water to boil; reduce heat to medium and remove surface debris. Add in 1 1/3 oz. (40g) dried bonito shavings (Fig. 2). Boil again; turn off heat and let stand 1 minute, then filter.

1 日式高湯燒開,加入 ¹ 料及調勻的 ² 料再燒開,撒上蔥花即成。

■ ¹ 料可任選蔬菜或海鮮取代。

■ **日式高湯:**將海帶 (10公分長,2片) 泡水 (8杯) 2-3小時,取出海帶 (圖1) 燒開,改中火去除泡沫,隨即放入柴魚1兩 (40公克,圖2) 再燒開立即熄火,靜置1分鐘過濾即成。

½ lb. (225g) presoftened shark's fin

1
½ t. salt
½ T. each: cooking wine, soy sauce
5 c. stock

乾魚翅（發好） ⋯⋯6兩（225公克）

1
鹽 ⋯⋯⋯⋯⋯⋯⋯⋯⋯⋯⋯¹/₂小匙
酒、醬油 ⋯⋯⋯⋯⋯⋯各¹/₂大匙
高湯 ⋯⋯⋯⋯⋯⋯⋯⋯⋯⋯⋯5杯

Shark's Fin Soup

魚翅湯

1 Blanch fin in boiling water 1 minute; remove.

2 Bring 1 to boil. Add shark's fin; bring to boil. Continue to cook 2 minutes. Serve. Add meat, bamboo shoots or Chinese black mushrooms as desired.

■ **TO SOFTEN DRIED FIN:** Soak fin in large volume of water overnight. Change the water then bring to boil. Reduce heat to medium and cook 10 minutes. Due to the variety of fins; some may need soaking and cooking several times before they are ready for final cooking.

1 發好的魚翅在滾水內川燙1分鐘後撈出。

2 將 1 料燒開，放入魚翅再燒開，續煮2分鐘即可，湯內可隨意加肉、筍、香菇絲等材料。

■ **乾魚翅發法：**乾魚翅先浸泡多量水隔夜，再換水燒開，改中火續煮10分鐘，魚翅因種類不同，有的需反覆的煮及泡水數次後才使用。

1
1 tomato, sliced
8 slices onion

2
7 T. sugar
5 T. lemon juice
4 c. ice water

3
8 slices lemon
ice cubes as desired

2 c. Dried white wood ears (agar-agar), presoftened in water

1
½ t. each: salt, sugar
pepper, sesame oil as desired
1 T. minced ginger root
5 c. chicken stock

1	番茄(切片)	1個
	洋蔥	8片

2	糖	7大匙
	檸檬汁	5大匙
	冰開水	4杯

3	檸檬	8片
	冰塊	適量

泡軟的白木耳	2杯

1	鹽、糖	各1/2小匙
	胡椒、麻油	各少許
	嫩薑(切碎)	1大匙
	雞高湯	5杯

Tomato and Onion Soup

洋蔥番茄涼湯

1 Soak **1** in cold water for 1 minute; remove. Add mixture **2** to **1** and refrigerate. Serve with **3**.

1 將 **1** 料用冷水泡1分鐘後撈出，加入拌勻的 **2** 料放冰箱冷藏，食用時加 **3** 料即可。夏天食用爽口。

White Wood Ear Broth

銀耳鷄湯

1 Clean and drain the wood ears.

2 Bring **1** to boil. Add wood ears; bring to boil. Reduce heat to medium and cook 20 minutes.

1 泡軟的白木耳洗淨，瀝乾水份。

2 將 **1** 料燒開，放入白木耳再燒開，改中火續煮20分鐘即成。

1 lb. (450g) ground beef

3 egg whites

1 c. water

1 | 1 small carrot, cut in pieces
1 celery, cut in pieces
1 small onion, cut in pieces

8 c. bouillon (see p. 7)

2 | ¾ T. unflavored gelatine
½ c. water

3 | ½ t. salt
1 t. soy sauce

瘦牛絞肉	………	12兩(450公克)
蛋白	………………………	3個
水	……………………………	1杯

1
紅蘿蔔(小，切塊) …………1條
西芹(切塊) …………………1支
洋蔥(小，切塊) ……………1個

西式高湯(見7頁)……………8杯

2
膠粉 ……………………3/4大匙
水 ……………………………1/2杯

3
鹽 ……………………………1/2小匙
醬油 ………………………1小匙

Beef in Aspic
琥珀牛肉凍羹

1 Mix egg whites then water with ground beef (Fig. 1). Mix in **1** (Fig. 2). Add bouillon and bring to boil; stir during cooking. Reduce heat to low; boil 1 hour. Cool then filter liquid to make stock.

2 Mix **2** and let stand 3 minutes until gelatine dissolves.

3 Bring stock to boil. Add **2** and **3**; turn off heat. Refrigerate one hour until solidified. Divide and put in 4 small bowls. Serve.

1 絞肉依序拌入蛋白、水(圖1)及 **1** 料(圖2)，隨入西式高湯邊煮邊攪至燒開，再降火候(小滾程度)不蓋鍋煮約1小時，待冷過濾即成精製高湯。

2 將 **2** 料攪拌浸泡3分鐘至膠粉溶化備用。

3 將精製高湯燒開，加 **2** 、 **3** 料即熄火，冷藏約1小時至凝固，分裝在碗內即成。

□ Index

□ 索引

More From Wei-Chuan Publishing 味全叢書

Cookbooks :
(All cookbooks are bilingual English/Chinese unless footnoted otherwise)

Chinese Appetizers & Garnishes
Chinese Cooking, Favorite Home Dishes [1]
Chinese Cooking For Beginners (Revised)
Chinese Cooking Made Easy
Chinese Cuisine
Chinese Cuisine-Szechwan Style.
Chinese Cuisine-Taiwanese Style
Chinese Dim Sum
Chinese One Dish Meals
Chinese Seafood [2]
Chinese Snacks (Revised)
Favorite Chinese Dishes
Great Garnishes
Healthful Cooking
Japanese Cuisine
Low Cholesterol Chinese Cuisine
Mexican Cooking Made Easy [3]
Microwave Cooking I, Chinese Style
Microwave Cooking II, Chinese Style
Noodles, Chinese Home-Cooking
Noodles, Classical Chinese Cooking
Rice, Chinese Home-Cooking
Rice, Traditional Chinese Cooking
Thai Cooking Made Easy
Vegetarian Cooking

Small Cookbook Series :
Vegetables [2]
Beef [2]
Chicken [2]
Tofu! Tofu! Tofu!
Very! Very! Vegetarian!
Soup! Soup! Soup!

Carving Tools

Videos [4] :
Chinese Garnishes I
Chinese Garnishes II
Chinese Stir-Frying, Beef
Chinese Stir-Frying, Chicken
Chinese Stir-Frying, Vegetables

1 Also available in English/Spanish, French/Chinese, and German/Chinese
2 English and Chinese are separate editions
3 Also available in English/Spanish
4 English only

食譜系列
(如無數字標註,即爲中英對照版)

拼盤與盤飾
實用家庭菜
實用中國菜 [1] (修訂版)
速簡中國菜
中國菜
四川菜
台灣菜
飲茶食譜
簡餐專輯
海鮮專輯 [2]
點心專輯
家常 100
盤飾精選
健康食譜
日本料理
均衡飲食
墨西哥菜 [3]
微波爐食譜
微波爐食譜 II
麵,家常篇
麵,精華篇
米食,家常篇
米食,傳統篇
泰國菜
素食

味全小食譜 :
牛肉 [2]
鷄肉 [2]
蔬菜 [2]
豆腐
家常素食
湯

雕花刀

錄影帶 [4]
盤飾 I
盤飾 II
炒菜入門,牛肉
炒菜入門,鷄肉
炒菜入門,蔬菜

1 中英、中法、中德、英西
2 中文版及英文版
3 中英版及英西版
4 英文版

Wei-Chuan Cookbooks can be purchased in the U.S.A., Canada and twenty other countries worldwide • Wei-Chuan Publishing • 1455 Monterey Pass Road, #1
Monterey Park, CA 91754, U.S.A. • Tel: (213)261-3880 • Fax: (213) 261-3299
味全食譜在台、美、加及全球二十餘國皆有發行 • 味全出版社有限公司 • 台北市仁愛路4段28號2樓 • Tel: (02) 702-1148 • Fax: (02) 704-2729